This book belongs to:

Given with Love by:

With a great big
Y a a a w n
and a stretch up to the sky,
it is time for our
nighttime lullaby.

Hush-a-bye, it's dreamy time.
Close your eyes and
# Yaaawn
Snuggle in and rest your head. You are safe in your bed.
Slow and soft, cozy and still, I love you now and I always will...
Goodnight Great Granddaughter, goodnight.

Chirp-chirp---chirp-chirp
A nighttime song they bring.

Deep in the trees, little birds rest in their nest gently tucking their heads next to their chest.

Puffy clouds float silently by,
Making their way across the dark night sky,
Listening as we slowly sing our nighttime lullaby.

Snuggle in and rest your head.
You are safe in your bed.
Slow and soft, cozy and still,
I love you now and I always will...
**Goodnight Great Granddaughter, goodnight.**

Deep in the woods the big black bears,
Crawl into their dens without a single care.

With a long sigh and a big-old-yawn,
They peek out and see a fawn.
She is snuggled in the green grass
Dreamy time is here at last.

Purrrr, purrrrr, purrr!
The kitten rests and admires
the warmth of the cozy crackling fire.

Purrrr, purrrrr, purrr!
the kitten sleeps as good dreams stir.
Purrrr, purrrrr, purrr!

The Milky Way stretches far and wide,
Reaching across the nighttime sky.

While shooting stars go racing past,
sleepy time is here at last.

The trees whisper quietly
in the cool night air,
Their leaves playing a
Gentle melody that is heard,
everywhere.

A quiet hush fills the night
as the world around us softly says,
goodnight.

Snuggle in and rest your head.
You are safe in your bed.
Slow and soft, cozy and still,

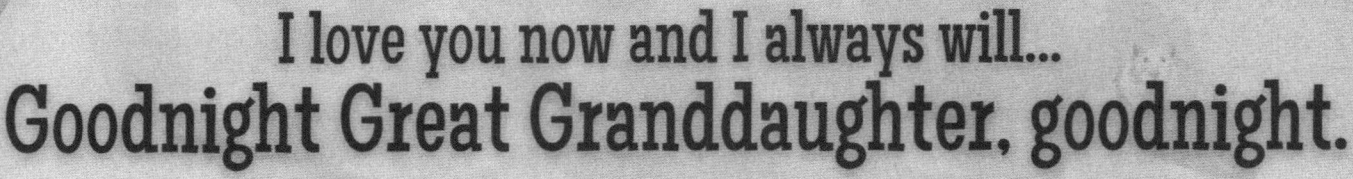

I love you now and I always will...
**Goodnight Great Granddaughter, goodnight.**

# The End

Printed in Dunstable, United Kingdom